Life-Cycle Stories

by Gladys Conklin:
CHIMPANZEE
GIRAFFE

by Marie M. Jenkins:
MOON JELLY

by William M. and Peggy Stephens:
FLAMINGO
HERMIT CRAB
KILLER WHALE
OCTOPUS
SEA HORSE
SEA TURTLE

by Donna E. DeSeyn:
TERMITE

by Elizabeth and Charles Schwartz:
BOBWHITE
COTTONTAIL RABBIT

by Barbara and Russell F. Peterson:
WHITEFOOT MOUSE

by Paul McCutcheon Sears:
BARN SWALLOW
DOWNY WOODPECKER
FIREFLY

by Mary Adrian:
FIDDLER CRAB
GARDEN SPIDER
GRAY SQUIRREL
HONEYBEE

by Marion W. Marcher:
MONARCH BUTTERFLY

*by William M. Stephens
and Peggy Stephens*

*illustrated by
Matthew Kalmenoff*

FLAMINGO

Bird
of
Flame

Holiday House · New York

To all lovers of Meher Baba
everywhere

A lone flamingo in the air is like a spurt of flame against the blue sky, and a flock of flamingos is as awe-inspiring as a tropical sunset. Those few ornithologists, or bird specialists, who have seen thousands of American flamingos on the nesting grounds at Great Inagua say there is no other sight like it in the bird kingdom.

Of the six kinds of flamingos in the world, the most brightly colored is the American flamingo (*Phoenicopterus ruber*), which is the subject of this book. This is the only flamingo that is really flaming red.

Anyone who wants to find out more about flamingos should read Robert Porter Allen's monumental work *The Flamingos: Their Life History and Survival.* For a short account of the European flamingo, *The Flamingos of the Camargue,* by Etienne Gallet, is highly recommended. Gallet's words are poetic, and his photographs are spectacular.

THE AUTHORS

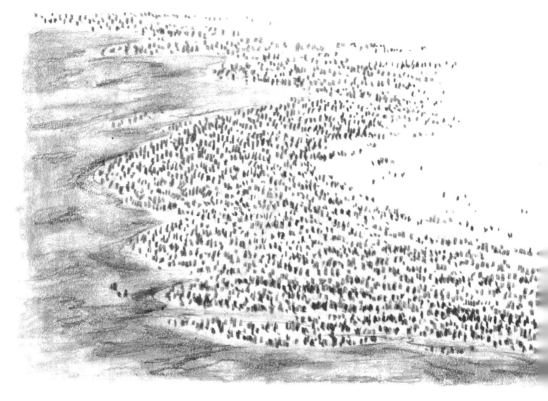

The Red Birds

If you could soar high over the island of Great
Inagua in the spring of the year, you would
see a rare sight. The salt lakes seem to be on
fire. A great cloud of blazing red rests on each
lake. The cloud is made up of many thousands
of flamingos wearing their brightest spring
colors. It is nesting time, and almost all the
flamingos from this part of the world are gathered here.

Most of the birds are sitting on little mounds of mud. Each mound looks like the stump of a tree. The mound is the flamingo's nest. Perched on the mound each adult bird sits in the hot sun with its legs folded beneath it. Among the birds are two that will soon be the parents of the chick Flamingo.

Great Inagua is over 500 miles southeast of Florida, in the Bahama Islands. The water around the island is deep and blue. Part of the land is rocky, hot and dry—almost like a desert. There is very little rainfall, and few plants can grow. Much of the island is swampy, with many shallow lakes bordered by man-grove trees. These trees stand high above the mud on long, curved roots.

Because of the lack of fresh water, not many people live at Great Inagua. But many thousands of birds live there. Most of them are flamingos.

There is very little water in the lakes. They are mostly mud, with layers of white salt that

have built up over hundreds of years as sea water dried away in the bright sun. Here and there are shallow puddles of water. When the tide is very high, sea water seeps into the lakes and covers much of the area with a thin sheet of water. After a few days, however, most of it has gone, and the mud may be dried and cracked by the sun.

Nests of Mud

Some of the nesting birds in this strange place have bent their long, slender necks into the form of a figure 8. This twisting helped them to smooth their feathers and clean lice from their skin. Other birds hid their heads under a wing as though asleep.

Some stretched their necks down to pick up a mouthful of wet mud and let it dribble down the outside of their mound. In this way they constantly built up and strengthened the mounds. The mud soon hardened in the dry air and became almost like concrete.

The mounds were only about two feet apart. When a bird stretched out its neck or spread its wings, it could easily touch one of its neighbors. From time to time a loud squawk of protest was heard when one bird caught another stealing mud from around its nest. Then the two birds hissed and honked and pecked at each other for a few minutes. Finally the clamor died down and they seemed to forget all about the matter.

At the day's end the rays of the setting sun cast long shadows across the great colony of flamingos. Then a big wave of red, like a forest fire, streaked over the tops of the mangrove trees and moved toward the lake from the sea. The approaching wave was a flock of flamingos —mates of those on the nests. They had been away feeding since early morning, and were ready to take their mates' places on the mounds.

The nesting birds screamed and flapped their wings. Some hopped up and stood on

top of their mounds, revealing a single large white egg they had been sitting on. Almost all the mounds had one egg. A few had two.

The arriving birds glided in and fluttered their big wings, stretched out their thin legs and landed. Each one alighted gracefully by its own nest. Then the birds that had been sitting on the nests hopped off. They honked and snorted and squawked, splashing about in the shallow pools of water.

Some stood in one place and shifted their weight back and forth from one leg to the other, as though exercising. Or they stretched their necks, first in one direction and then in another. Many of them beat their wings as they got ready to take off.

Soon a flight of a few hundred birds headed for a feeding ground in one of the shallow lagoons surrounding Great Inagua. Another group of birds flew off in a different direction, to a different lagoon. Some went to other islands to feed. But all would return in the morning to take their mates' places on the nests.

The birds on the ground were now getting set for the night. Many were hopping onto their mound and rolling the egg over or turning it around with their bills. They did this to line up the egg with their body before sitting on it. Some of the birds scooped up a mouthful of water from a nearby puddle and washed the egg. This may have helped keep the egg clean, or perhaps cooled it.

After a time most of the birds settled on their nests for the night. But other flamingos, in smaller groups, arrived from different places to relieve their mates. At almost any time, day or night, a few birds were arriving or leaving.

And there was always noise to disturb these gentle days of May. Peace and silence are never found in a flamingo colony. From nearby, the sound was much like a loud and busy barnyard. From far away it sounded more like a chorus of frogs.

Flamingo Hatches

In June the first eggs began to hatch. Inside one of these eggs, Flamingo started to struggle against his hard prison. His voice came out in muffled peeps.

Escaping from the egg would be a long and painful process. While Flamingo pushed,

pecked, pulled, and struggled, his mother stood by the mound and watched. She was helpless to aid her chick but she kept her head next to the egg, waiting for him to come out.

After a crack appeared on the lower side of the egg, his mother rolled it over so that the crack was up. Soon Flamingo's tiny head and short bill pushed through the break. He struggled hard to pull the rest of his body through.

For a while he seemed to be in danger of being strangled by the egg. While he wriggled and squirmed, the egg rolled back and forth, until it almost toppled off the mound. Finally one stubby wing came through, and one foot. Then he was free. Flamingo lay on his side, wet, helpless, and exhausted, beside the broken eggshell.

As Flamingo's small body was warmed and dried by the morning sun, his outer covering became white and fluffy. Now he was ready for his first meal, which was dribbled from his mother's beak. Later his father would feed him in the same way.

The food of a newborn flamingo chick is a dark liquid produced in both parents by special glands. Flamingo's mother pushed the tip of her large bill into her chick's open mouth and let a few drops of the liquid flow down his throat.

A little later Flamingo had his second meal. He ate the eggshell from which he had hatched—every piece of it. The shell con-

tained important minerals that would help his body to grow.

Flamingo and the hundreds of other chicks did not look at all like their parents. The chicks' legs, bills, and necks were very short, and their bills were not at all curved like those of the adults. They were almost as noisy as their parents, but the noise was very different. The chicks made a mewing or chirping sound. Sometimes they sounded like any other kind of baby bird. At other times they sounded like kittens. All of them were very active.

After a few hours Flamingo suddenly fell out of the nest. He struggled in the mud below, trying to crawl up the side of the mound and get back onto it. Other chicks that had fallen stood huddled next to their mounds while one of their parents stretched down its long neck and fed them. After many tries, Flamingo reached the top of his mound again.

Within a week Flamingo and some of the other chicks were wandering around the col-

ony in large groups, chirping constantly, running and falling in the mud, and sometimes swimming in the deeper puddles of water. Other chicks were being born every day, and many of the eggs had not hatched yet.

Getting His Food

So many chicks were in the colony now that when a flight of adult birds arrived, the chicks ran and stumbled and fell all over the place as they begged for food. Perhaps the adult birds knew which were their own chicks; or perhaps they just fed the chick that reached them first.

By the time he was two weeks old, Flamingo was finding much of his own food. He fed by dipping his head in shallow water or wet mud. He took a mouthful of mud or water and used his tongue to force it out through strainers at the sides of his mouth. He swallowed tiny snails, brine shrimp, and other creatures trapped by the strainers, along with some of the mud. A great many plants too small to see lived in the mud and made up a large part of the food.

His parents would continue to feed Flamingo from time to time for several weeks, but soon he would get most of his food on his own.

Flamingo's jaws were now growing longer. Also, the end of his bill had begun to curve downward. His legs also were growing longer, and he could run very fast. Whenever he and the other chicks were startled by a shadow overhead, they ran as fast as they could toward the nearest puddle. In the flamingo colony there was practically no cover or shade of any

kind and no place to hide if danger threatened.

Fortunately, the flamingos had few enemies. Now and then a hawk, man-of-war bird, or gull would drift over, and sometimes a wild hog would come to gobble up any dead or injured birds it could find. But such attacks were rare. The nesting grounds were located in such an uncomfortable place that not many other animals came near. Few animals other than flamingos could stay alive in such a hot, salty place with no fresh water.

When Flamingo was about a month old, he began to turn gray. Dark feathers came in to replace the white down that covered his body at birth. Now he often stood and waved his stubby wings to exercise his muscles. Soon a few pink feathers appeared, and some black and brown ones. His legs, which were red at birth, had now turned brown. Later they would become red again. At six weeks of age he was blotchy all over and looked more like a scarecrow than a flamingo.

A Giant Metal Bird

One day all the birds in the colony were
startled by a loud rumbling sound. Then a
great shadow passed over. It was an airplane
carrying tourists from Haiti who came to see
the flamingos. As the plane swooped low over
the colony, the birds became wildly excited.

All the adults took flight and disappeared over the mangrove trees.

None of the chicks could fly yet, and they ran this way and that, not knowing where to go. Many of the younger ones were trampled and crushed. Some of them stuck their heads in the mud to try to get away from the loud noise of the plane. Some birds plunged into the water. Others just stood still, shaking.

After the plane left, many of the injured birds were caught and eaten by two wild hogs that were attracted by the disturbance. They fed hungrily, rooting about in the mud, until some of the adult flamingos returned to the colony and drove the hogs away. Some of the adult birds did not return to the colony, but flew to other islands.

Learning To Fly

After Flamingo was about eight weeks old he spent much of his time trying to fly. Flapping his wings, he would jump off mounds. And he would run through the mud, taking long strides and trying to push himself up into the air. All over the colony young flamingos were

racing up and down and jumping. Often they knocked others into a spin or trampled on one another.

Finally, when they were about eleven weeks old, they began actually to fly. They rose gracefully in the air with their necks pushed straight out like a spear and their legs trailing behind.

Often Flamingo took a spill while landing, but he was never hurt. A bad landing merely meant a tumble in the mud or the shallow water. He learned rapidly and was soon flying perfectly, soaring high and gliding over the mangroves to feed in lagoons along the shore.

He now had learned to feed like the adult birds. Walking backward in shallow water, he curved his neck down so that his upper bill went beneath the water and acted like a scoop to shovel up mud and sediment. In the lagoons, where many small animals lived, the birds sometimes fed on tiny fishes, crabs, and other kinds of food they could not find in the salt lakes.

The Storm

When Flamingo was about four months old, a hurricane formed in the southern Bahamas, not far from Great Inagua. The strong winds whipped up high waves, and sea water began flooding the colony. The adult birds all took flight and left the island. Flamingo and other

young birds that were old enough to fly fol-
lowed them, winging out over the dark seas
in an effort to escape the storm.

Some of the younger chicks were not yet able to fly. Others were just learning and did not have enough skill and strength to travel far over open water. Most of these chicks were killed when a high storm wave swept through the entire colony, drowning hundreds of chicks and washing away the mounds.

Flamingo and many of the other birds stayed alive by waiting out the storm in huddled groups on a high island they reached after flying for several hours. The island was Cuba, only about fifty miles from Great Inagua, across the deep water that lies between the southern Bahamas and the West Indies. This was Flamingo's first visit to Cuba. In years to come he would often fly to distant parts of the island, sometimes to stay for months, feeding in its lagoons.

After the storm passed, some of the birds returned to Great Inagua. Others remained in Cuba or flew to low islands in the southern

Bahamas. By the end of the year the flamingo flocks were fairly well scattered.

Then in January they all began winging their way back to their homeland. By February thousands of birds had gathered at Great Inagua. While the adult birds mated and built nests, Flamingo and the other yearlings watched. Next year they would be ready to become parents too. In the meantime they played at building mounds and nests, just as children play house.

Almost Grown Up

By the time nesting began, Flamingo had grown to look almost exactly like an adult bird. His feathers were now mostly bright red and pink. The upper part of his bill and his eye were yellow, and the rear parts of his wings were solid black.

After the nesting season was over and many of the adult birds flew away, Flamingo left too. He flew with a group of birds to a very small deserted island. They remained there for months, feeding in the rich, shallow waters of the lagoon. While they were there, Flamingo began molting—his feathers started to fall out. A few at a time dropped and new feathers soon sprouted. But for a few weeks, while his flight feathers were falling, he could not fly. For the rest of his life this would happen to him every year after the nesting season. Before the molting he would always fly to a distant place where he would be safe.

The following year when the birds came to Great Inagua in February, Flamingo was a fully grown bird, ready to mate. He was now almost two years old, five feet tall and perfectly developed. He joined thousands of other birds as they milled about, preparing for the mating dance.

Finally the male birds began walking stiffly with their legs straight and their wings out. Some turned their heads upside down.

Each male seemed to be trying to outdo the others. Flamingo strutted and pranced as he displayed his brilliant feathers.

Flamingo's Mate

While this was going on, the females walked slowly about with their heads down and their bills trailing in the water. Finally one of the males selected a mate and leaped at her. Flamingo spotted a young female and approached her. She signaled to him by crouching low in the shallow water. Then Flamingo leaped on her back and thrust his feet under her wings. After a few seconds the mating was completed. Now Flamingo and his mate stayed together every moment.

Within a few days the two of them began building a mound. They dug a circular canal with their bills and heaped the mud up in a mound in the center. Gradually the mound grew higher and higher. At the top they scraped out a low place for the egg to rest. Then Flamingo's mate sat on the nest and laid the egg.

For the next thirty days she and Flamingo took turns sitting on the egg night and day. One of them was always with the egg while the other was away feeding. After the egg hatched, the two would feed and watch their chick until it was old enough to get its own food.

Flamingo and his mate would spend many years among the beautiful islands of the Bahamas. Since they had few natural enemies, they might live for 75 or 80 years and produce many young flamingos to lend beauty and grace to shallow lagoons of the tropical Atlantic.